The NYSTROM Map Champ ATLAS

NYSTROM

DIVISION OF HERFF JONES, INC.

Executive Editor	Charles Novosad
Atlas and Map Design	Matthew V. Kania
Project Manager	Joan Pederson
Cartographic Manager	Christine D. Bosacki
Managing Editor	Ruth P. Koval
Cartoon Illustrations	Jackie Urbanovic
Map Compilation	Michael Nauert
Nystrom Computer Cartography	Phyllis Kawano
	Bonnie Jones
	Charlaine Wilkerson
Photographic Research	Susana Darwin
Cover Design	The Quarasan Group, Inc.
Logo Design	Bruce Hendrickson
Educational Consultant	Dr. JoAnne Buggey

For information about ordering this atlas, call toll-free 800-621-8086.

10 9 8 7 6 5 4   00 99 98

ISBN: 0-7825-0637-2   Product Code Number: 9A97C
Printed in U.S.A.

Contents

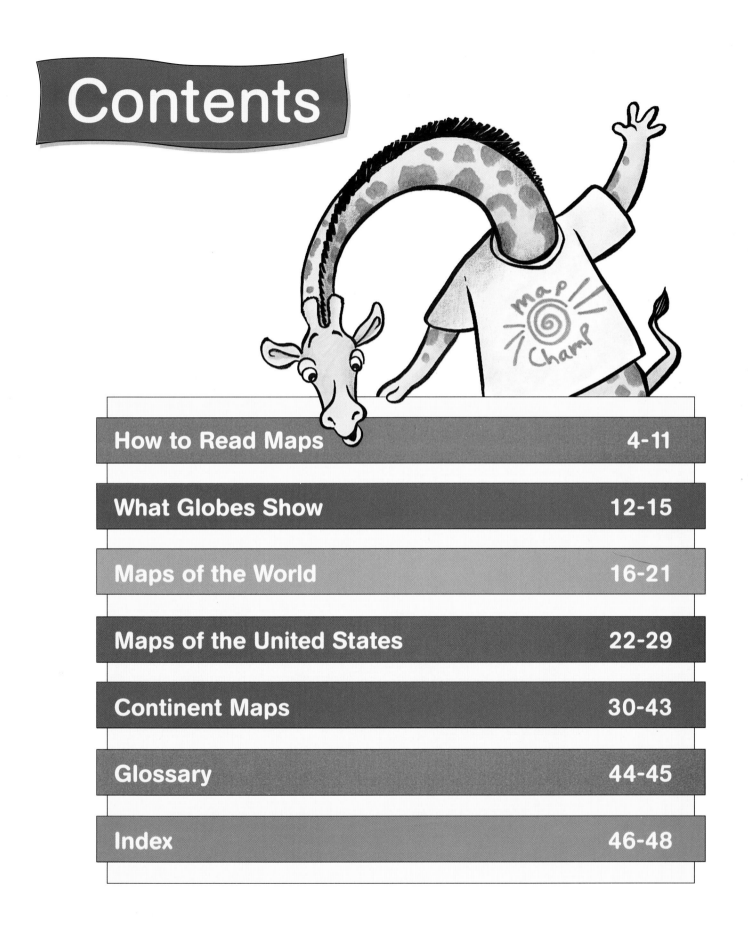

What is a map?

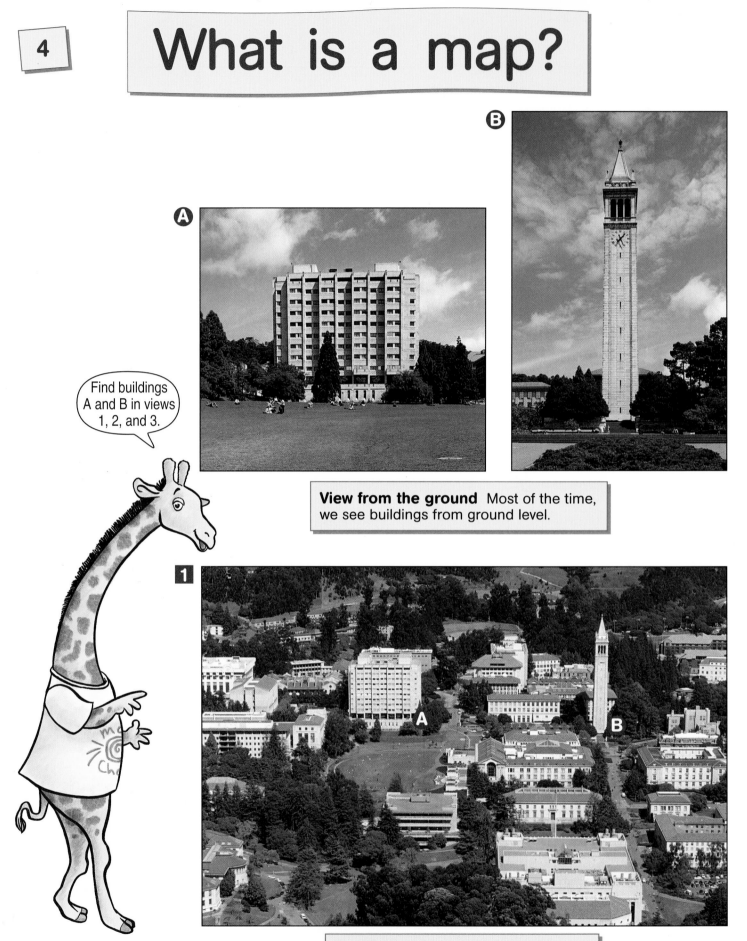

Find buildings A and B in views 1, 2, and 3.

View from the ground Most of the time, we see buildings from ground level.

Bird's-eye view This is how the same buildings might look to a bird in flight.

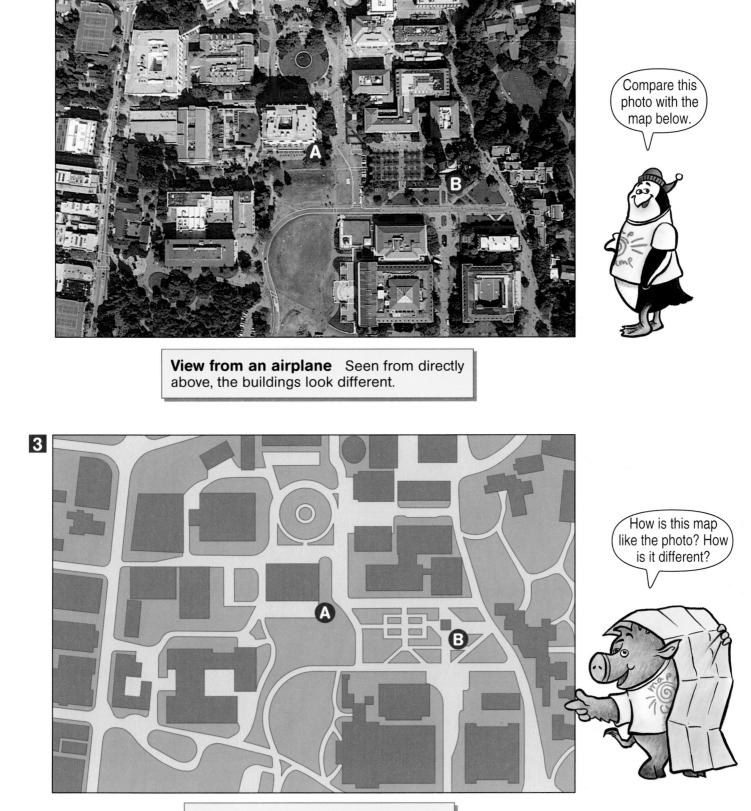

2

Compare this photo with the map below.

View from an airplane Seen from directly above, the buildings look different.

3

How is this map like the photo? How is it different?

Map view A map is a special drawing of an area as seen from directly above.

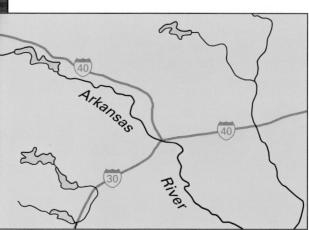

Highways Maps show highways as lines with names or numbers.

Railroads How is the railroad symbol different from the real thing?

Map symbols are a kind of picture code.

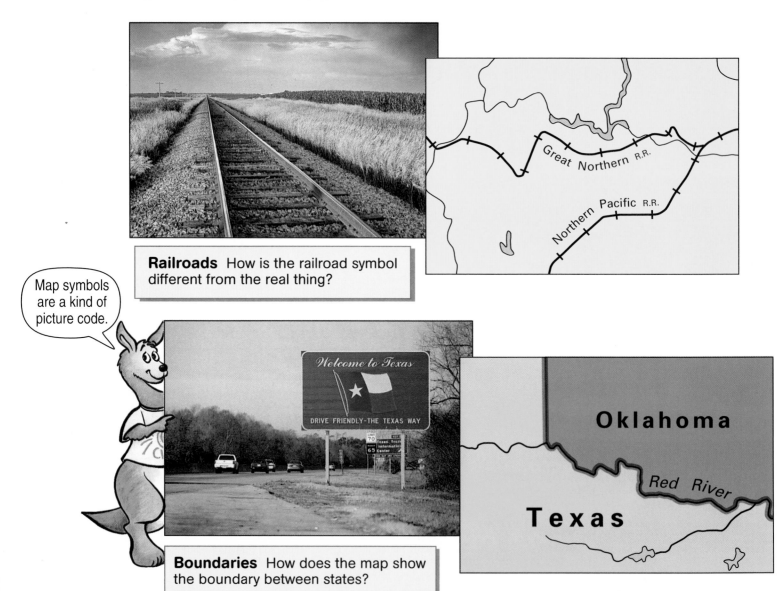

Boundaries How does the map show the boundary between states?

real world?

Swamps The symbol for a swamp looks like the grasses that grow there.

Everglades

Some symbols look like what they stand for.

Deserts Many deserts are sandy. What does the symbol remind you of?

Sonoran Desert

Symbols make the real world look simple.

Cities Dots show where cities are located. Stars show capital cities.

Mississippi

Minneapolis   St. Paul

Minnesota River   River

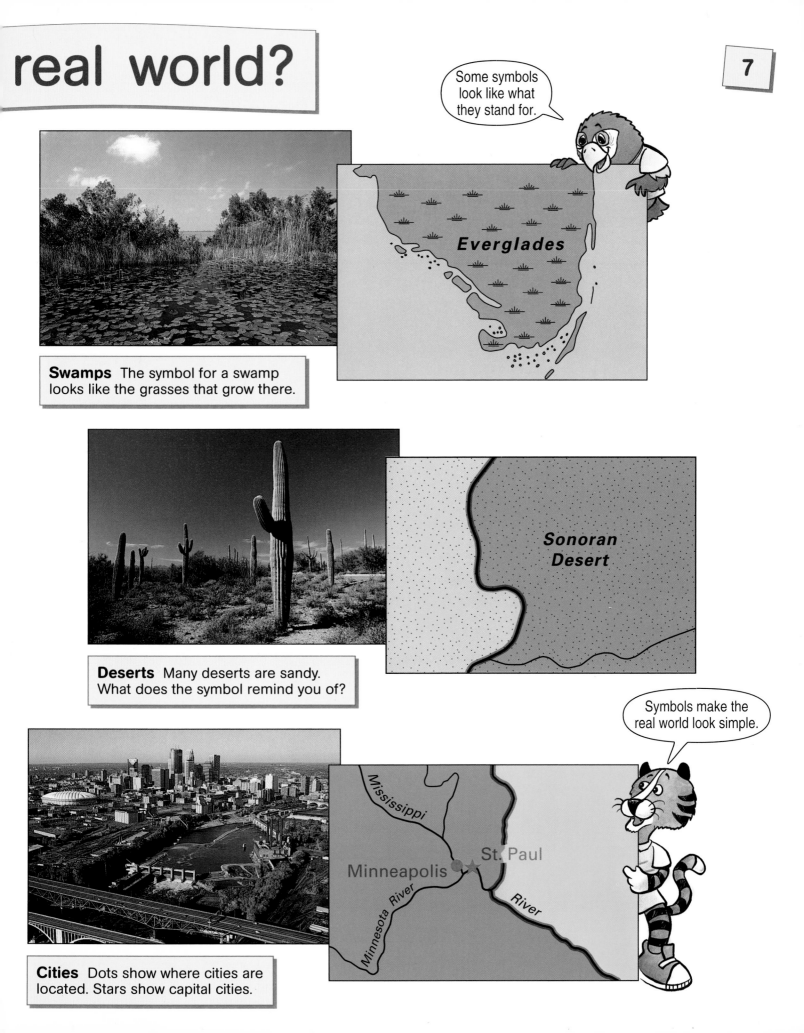

How are colors used as

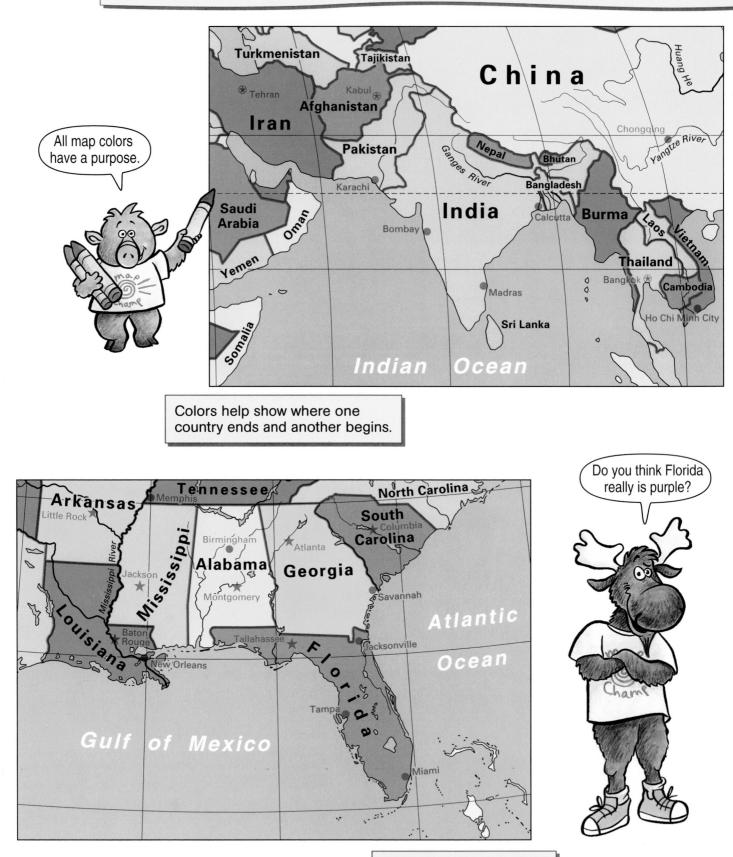

All map colors have a purpose.

Colors help show where one country ends and another begins.

Do you think Florida really is purple?

On this map, colors mark states, not countries.

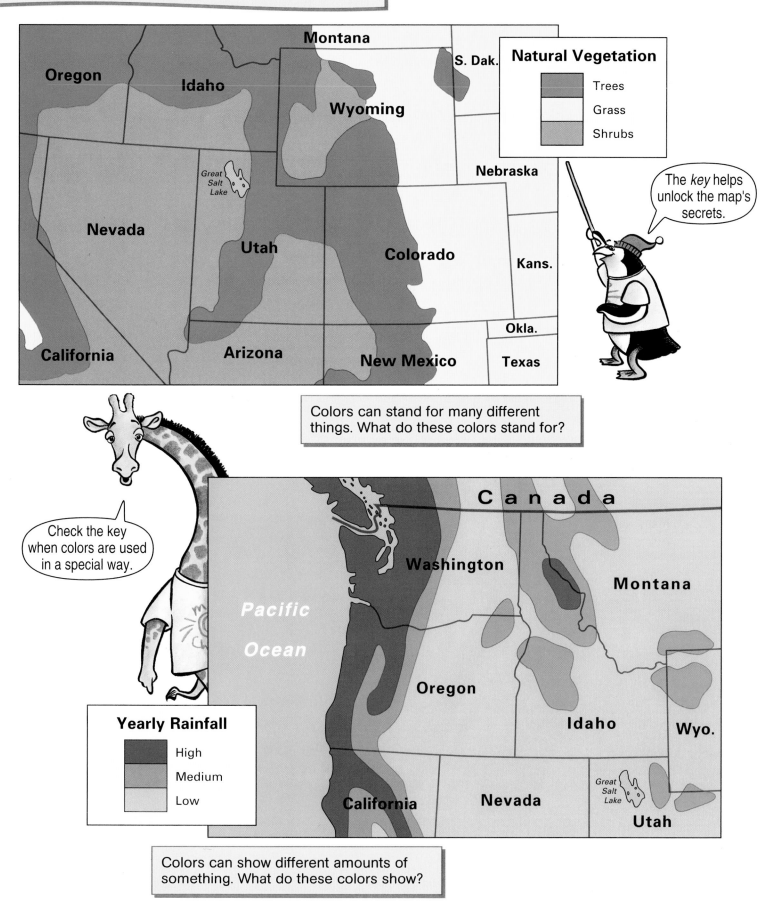

Natural Vegetation

- Trees
- Grass
- Shrubs

The *key* helps unlock the map's secrets.

Colors can stand for many different things. What do these colors stand for?

Check the key when colors are used in a special way.

Yearly Rainfall

- High
- Medium
- Low

Colors can show different amounts of something. What do these colors show?

Mount Fuji is a famous mountain in Japan. Can you find its snowy peak on the map?

A chain of mountains is called a *range.*

Maps can show mountains in many ways.

Compare the mountain shadows in the photo with the "shadows" on the map.

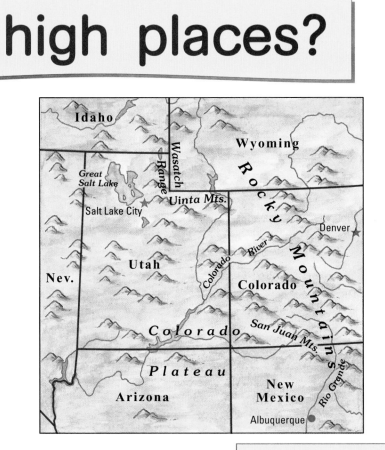

Some map symbols have mountain shapes.
Others imitate mountain shadows.

**Major Mountain Ranges
of the United States**

What is a globe?

You have to go WAY up for this view!

Seen from space, the earth looks like a big, blue marble.

Adding lines helps us tell land from water.

Only a few astronauts have gone high enough to see that the earth really is round.

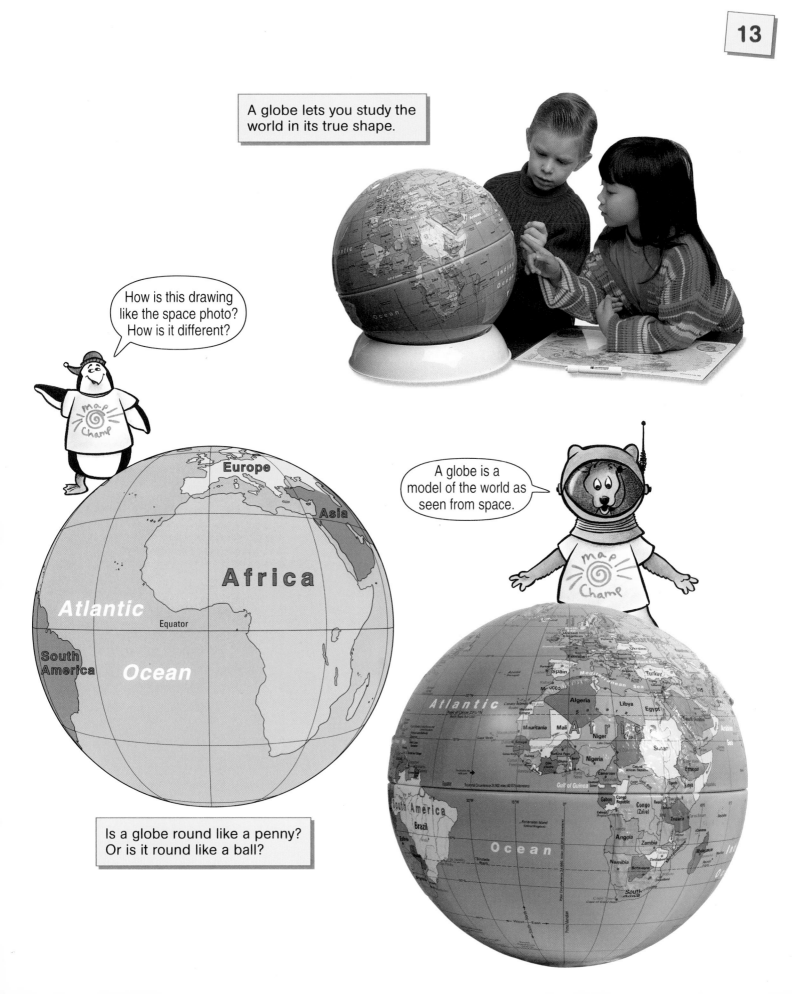

How are maps and globes

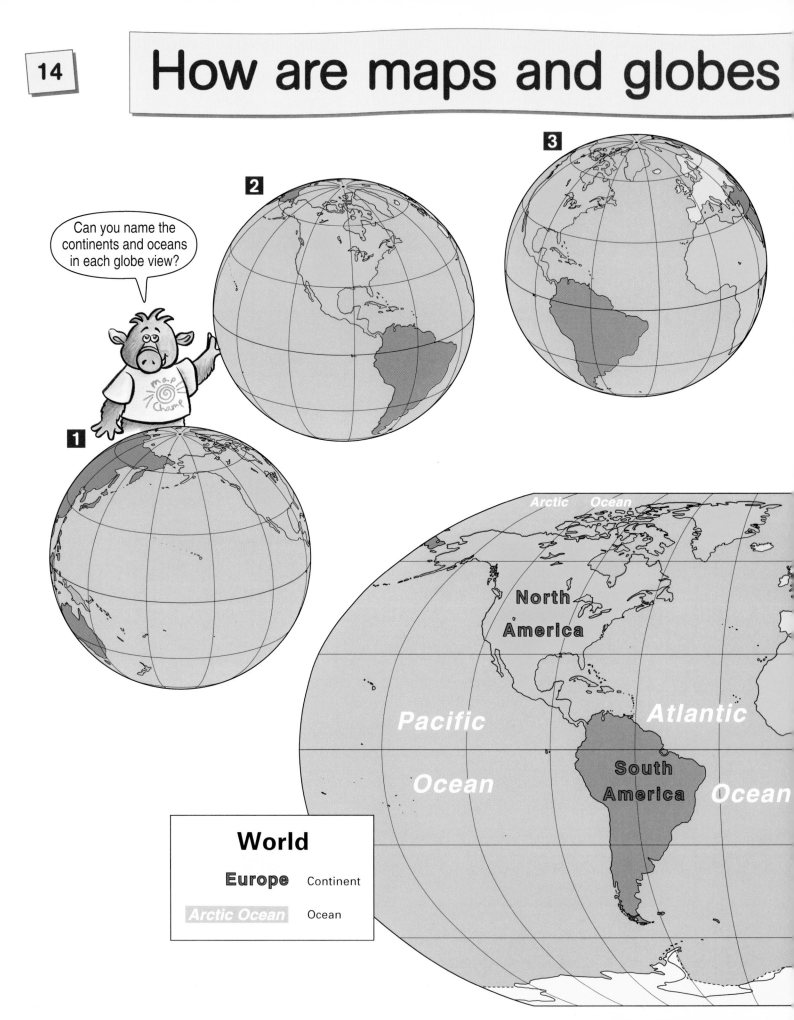

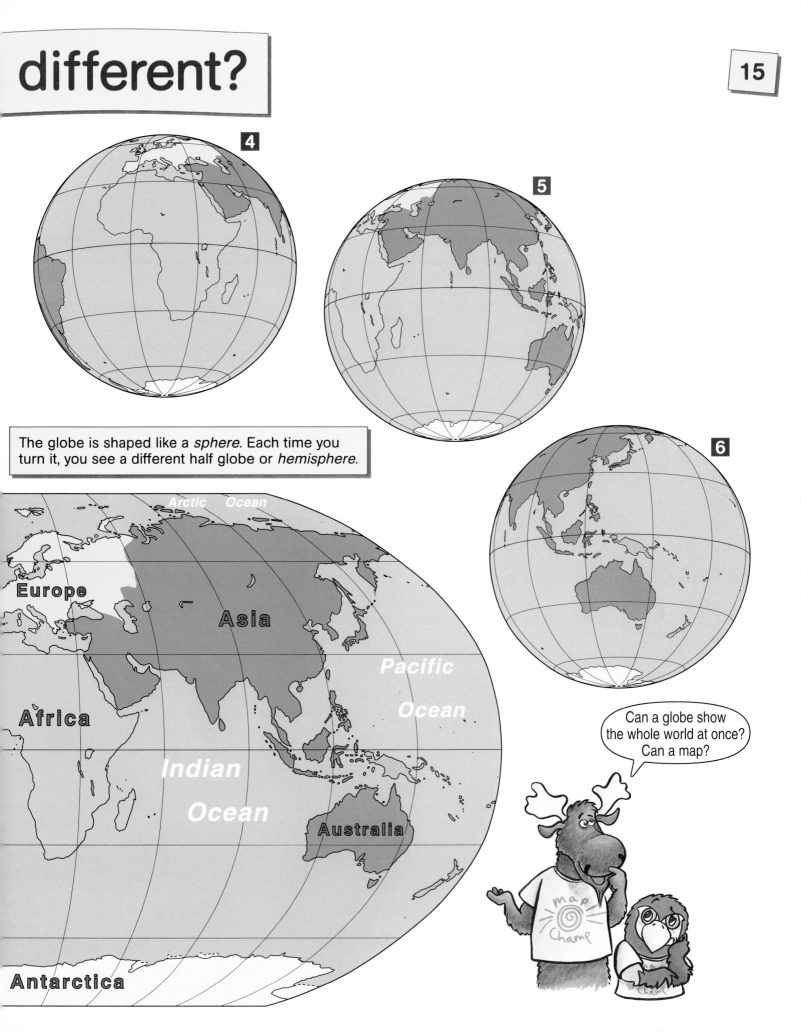

The globe is shaped like a *sphere*. Each time you turn it, you see a different half globe or *hemisphere*.

Can a globe show the whole world at once? Can a map?

Which are continents and

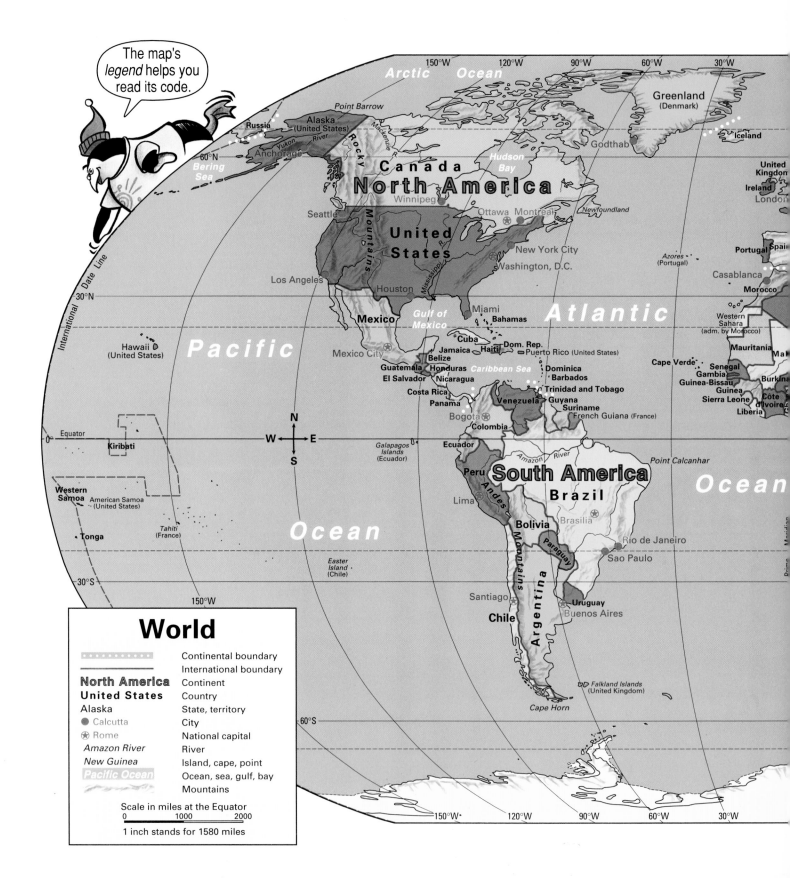

The map's *legend* helps you read its code.

World

··········	Continental boundary
————	International boundary
North America	Continent
United States	Country
Alaska	State, territory
● Calcutta	City
✪ Rome	National capital
Amazon River	River
New Guinea	Island, cape, point
Pacific Ocean	Ocean, sea, gulf, bay
	Mountains

Scale in miles at the Equator

0   1000   2000

1 inch stands for 1580 miles

Use the *compass rose* to find directions on the map.

Which continent is also a country?

Where in the world do

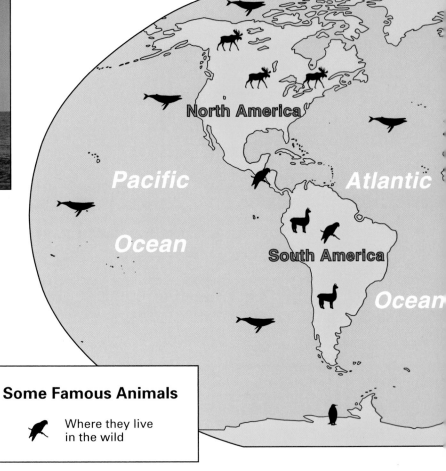

Arctic Ocean

North America

Pacific

Ocean

Atlantic

South America

Ocean

Some Famous Animals

Where they live
in the wild

Whale

Moose

Parrot

Llama

Penguin

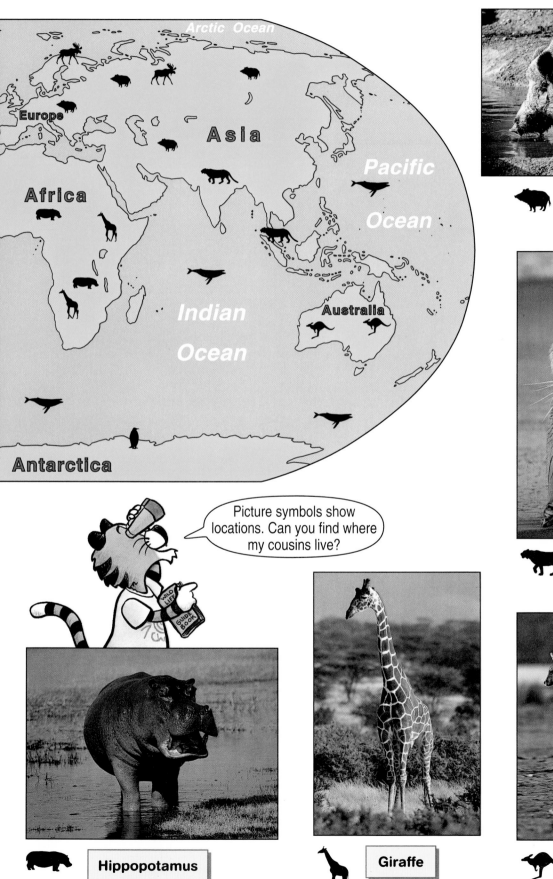

Wild Boar

Tiger

Kangaroo

Picture symbols show locations. Can you find where my cousins live?

Hippopotamus

Giraffe

Which places are hot and

A In which season do leaves change color and fall from the trees?

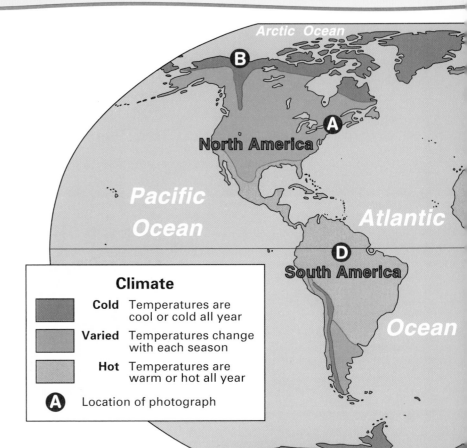

Arctic Ocean

B

A

North America

Pacific Ocean

Atlantic

D

South America

Ocean

Climate

Cold Temperatures are cool or cold all year

Varied Temperatures change with each season

Hot Temperatures are warm or hot all year

A Location of photograph

B Inuit children in Alaska play with a home-made sled.

C A shepherd's clothes help protect him from the hot sun in Egypt.

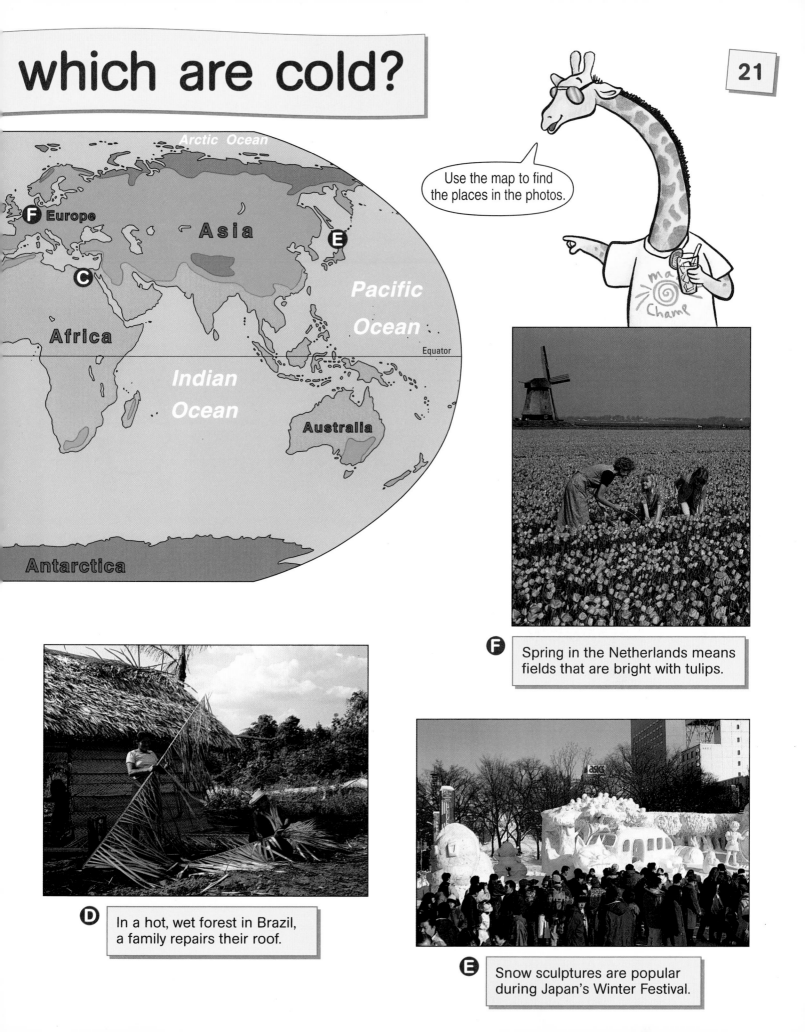

which are cold?

Use the map to find the places in the photos.

Arctic Ocean

F Europe

Asia

C

E

Pacific Ocean

Africa

Equator

Indian Ocean

Australia

Antarctica

F Spring in the Netherlands means fields that are bright with tulips.

D In a hot, wet forest in Brazil, a family repairs their roof.

E Snow sculptures are popular during Japan's Winter Festival.

Where in the world is the

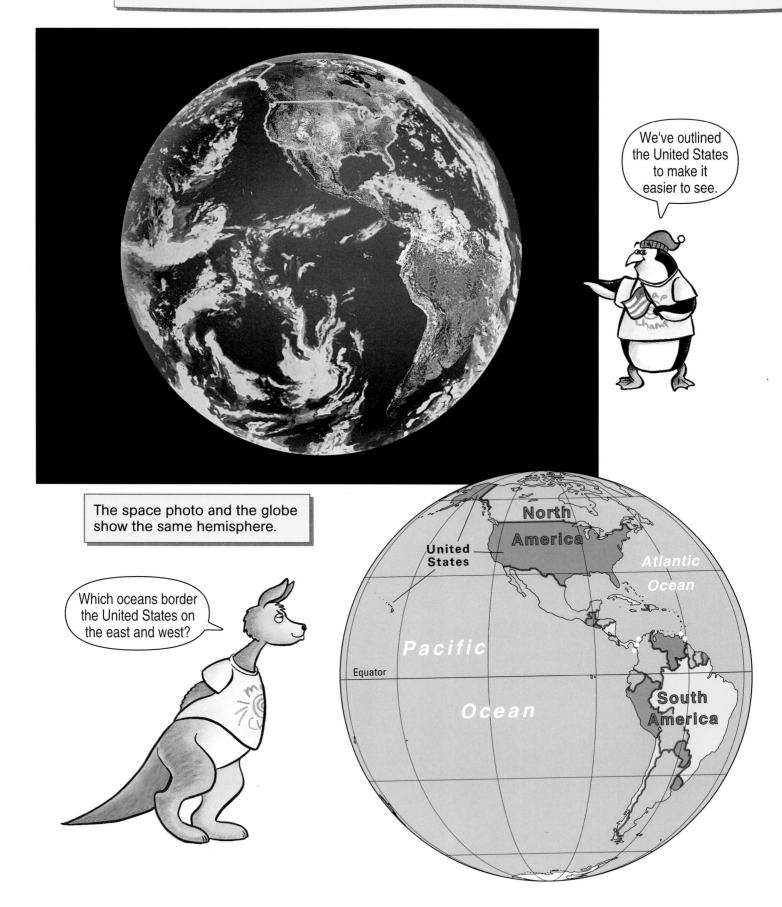

We've outlined the United States to make it easier to see.

The space photo and the globe show the same hemisphere.

Which oceans border the United States on the east and west?

Which continent is the United States part of?

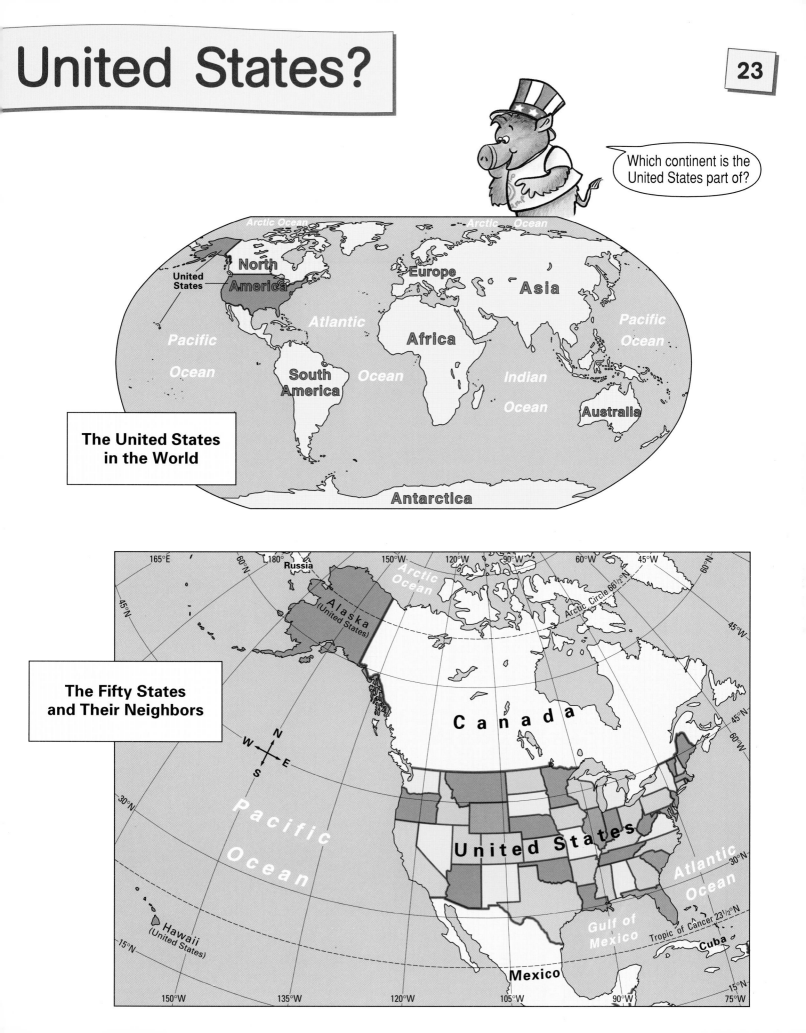

The United States in the World

The Fifty States and Their Neighbors

Can you find your state?

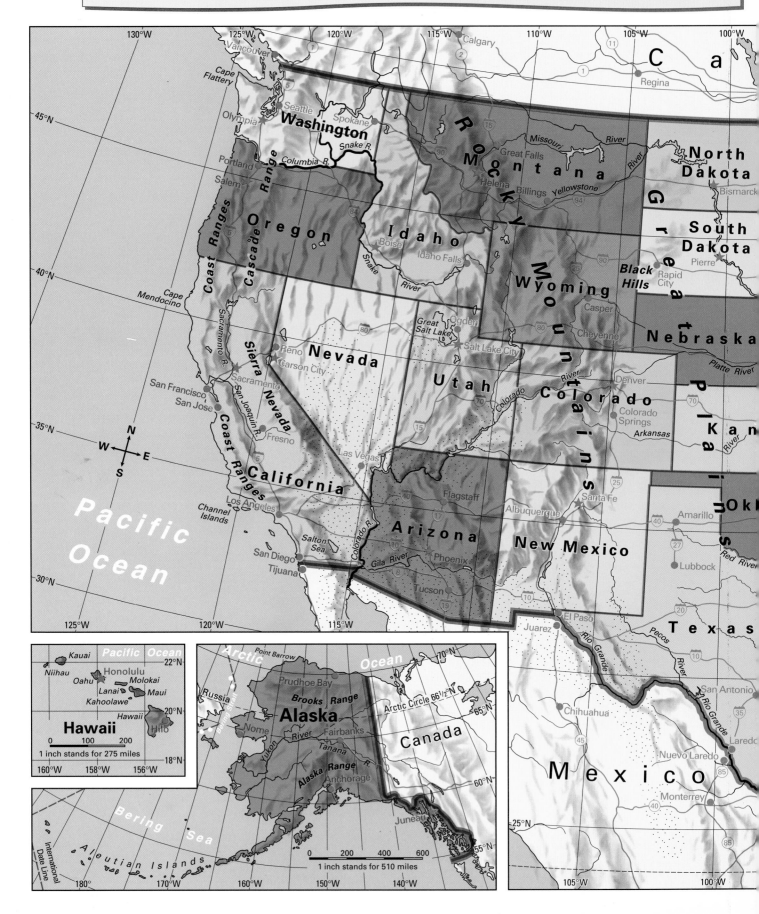

Washington · Oregon · Idaho · Montana · North Dakota · South Dakota

Rocky Mountains · Great Plains

Nevada · Utah · Wyoming · Colorado · Nebraska · Kansas

California · Arizona · New Mexico · Texas

Pacific Ocean

Hawaii — 1 inch stands for 275 miles

Alaska — 1 inch stands for 510 miles

Mexico

United States

∙∙∙∙∙∙∙∙∙	Continental boundary
▬▬▬▬	International boundary
———	State boundary
Mexico	Country
Arizona	State
● New York City	City
⊛ Washington, D.C.	National capital
★ Olympia	State capital
Snake River	River, lake, island, cape
Pacific Ocean	Ocean, sea, gulf
	Desert
	Swamp
	Mountains
—90—	Interstate highway

Scale in miles

0   100   200   300   400

1 inch stands for 225 miles

How do people use the

Find Alaska and Hawaii on this map and on page 23.

Land Use

Big city and its suburbs
Farming
Ranching
Forestry
Little or no use

Ⓐ Location of photograph

Ⓐ **Forestry** means growing and cutting trees for wood products.

Ⓑ **Ranching** means raising large herds of cattle or sheep.

Ⓒ **Little or no use** means land that is too wet, dry, or cold for much use.

What do these map colors stand for? Check the map's title and key.

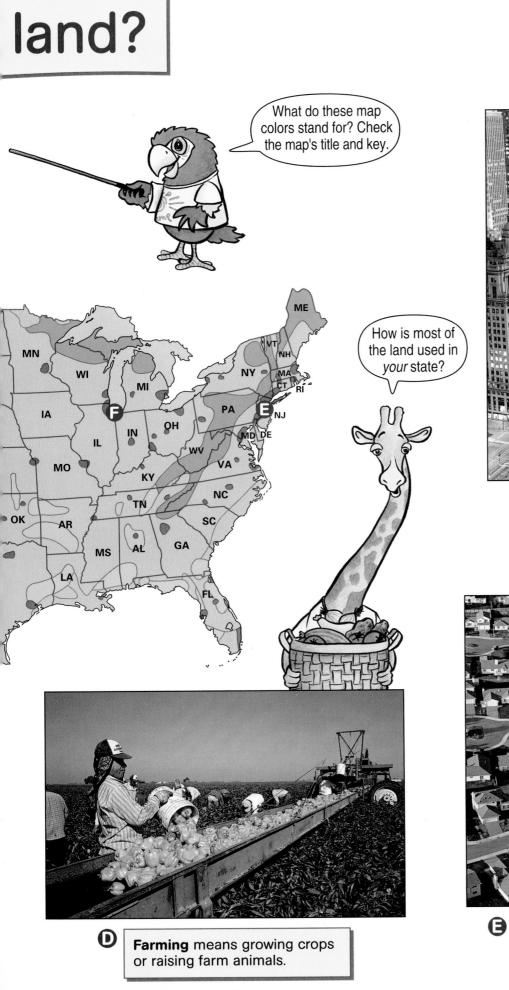

How is most of the land used in *your* state?

F **Big cities** have many tall buildings where people live and work.

D **Farming** means growing crops or raising farm animals.

E **Suburbs** are towns and small cities near a big city.

What are some special

A Yosemite National Park

B Olympic National Park

National Parks and Forests

- National Parks
- National Forests
- Other parks
- **A** Location of photograph

C Grand Canyon National Park

D Yellowstone National Park

H Isle Royale National Park

G Acadia National Park

E Great Smoky Mountains National Park

F Biscayne National Park

What is it like to live in

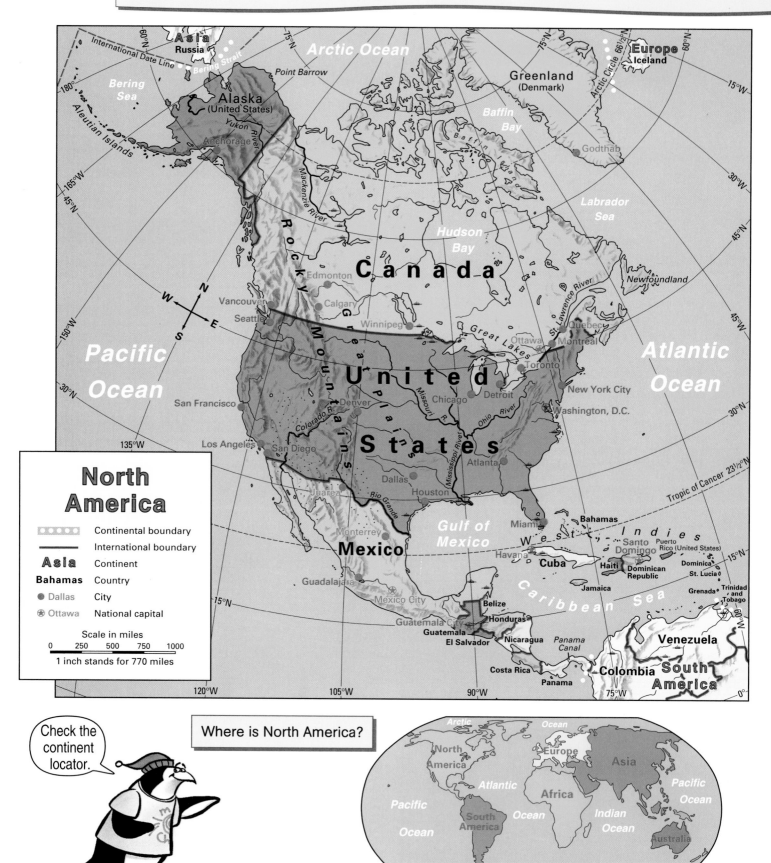

North America

Continental boundary
········

International boundary
────

Asia Continent

Bahamas Country

● **Dallas** City

✳ **Ottawa** National capital

Scale in miles
0 250 500 750 1000

1 inch stands for 770 miles

Check the continent locator.

Where is North America?

North America?

How is life in the rest of North America like life in the United States?

For this farm family near Winnipeg, Canada, the main crop is wheat.

In Mexico City, drivers face traffic jams every rush hour.

A Cuban farm worker cuts sugar cane by hand.

Can you guess the most popular sport in Mexico?

Shoppers in Guatemala buy yarn to weave into colorful clothing.

South America

Legend:
- •••••• Continental boundary
- —— International boundary
- **North America** Continent
- **Paraguay** Country
- ● Sao Paulo City
- ✼ Caracas National capital

Scale in miles
0 250 500 750 1000
1 inch stands for 700 miles

Where is South America?

How does the map show national capitals?

South America?

A front porch becomes a gym for a boy in Brazil.

Newer apartments rise above older houses in Caracas, Venezuela.

How is life in South America like life here?

A farm family in Peru harvests their potato crop.

Fishermen in Chile prepare to sell their day's catch.

In Argentina, he's a gaucho. We would call him a cowboy.

What is it like to live in

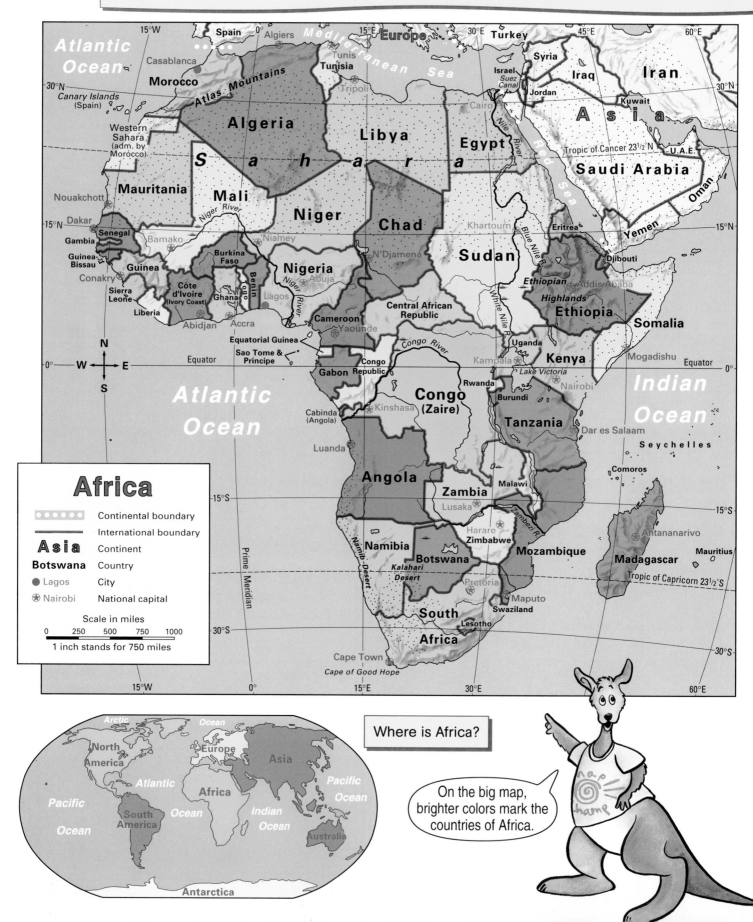

Africa

○○○○○○	Continental boundary
——	International boundary
Asia	Continent
Botswana	Country
● Lagos	City
✳ Nairobi	National capital

Scale in miles

0   250   500   750   1000

1 inch stands for 750 miles

Where is Africa?

On the big map, brighter colors mark the countries of Africa.

Africa?

Mining gold in South Africa is hot, noisy work.

In Cairo, Egypt, a fruit seller prepares fresh juice.

Which ocean is to the east?
Which one is to the west?

This Masai family herds cattle on Kenya's grasslands.

A girl in Togo babysits her younger sister.

In parts of Mali, the best way to travel is by boat.

What is it like to live in

London, in the United Kingdom, is one of Europe's many big cities.

What does the Spanish word *frutas* mean?

Where is Europe?

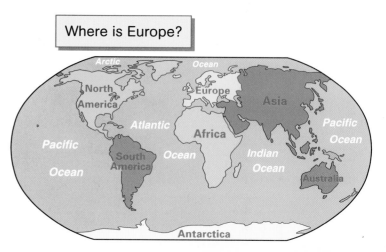

Follow Europe's coastline and name its seas.

Europe?

Europe

○○○○○	Continental boundary
——	International boundary
Asia	Continent
Ukraine	Country
● Istanbul	City
✪ Berlin	National capital

Scale in miles

0   250   500   750

1 inch stands for 425 miles

Part of Russia is in another continent. Which one?

In Germany, a farm family harvests their grapes.

A French girl brings fresh bread home from the bakery.

Many Russians and other Europeans work in factories.

Elephants are still used as work animals in Thailand.

Like these students on a school trip, most people in Japan use trains.

Are the north-south and east-west lines straight or curved?

Where is Asia?

Asia?

Asia

⬠⬠⬠⬠⬠⬠	Continental boundary
——————	International boundary
Africa	Continent
Thailand	Country
⬤ Karachi	City
✺ Baghdad	National capital

Scale in miles

0   250   500   750   1000

1 inch stands for 950 miles

At a market in Kazakstan, fruit is weighed before it is sold.

How is recess at this school in China like recess at yours?

Is more of Russia in Asia or in Europe?

An Indian family goes to visit their relatives.

What is it like to live in

Ayers Rock is a favorite site for families on vacation.

Most Australians live near the ocean in cities like Sydney.

Who won? Junior lifeguards compete in a game at the beach.

Where is Australia?

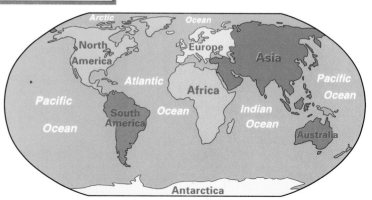

What is the map's *scale* in miles?

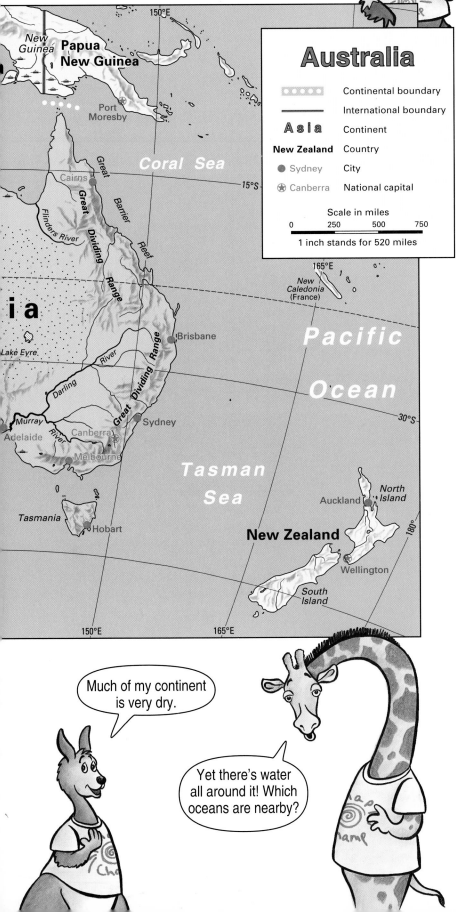

Australia

⬜⬜⬜⬜⬜	Continental boundary
———	International boundary
Asia	Continent
New Zealand	Country
● Sydney	City
✴ Canberra	National capital

Scale in miles

0   250   500   750

1 inch stands for 520 miles

Some ranchers use motorcycles to herd their sheep.

What does this sign warn drivers to watch for?

Much of my continent is very dry.

Yet there's water all around it! Which oceans are nearby?

Does anyone really live

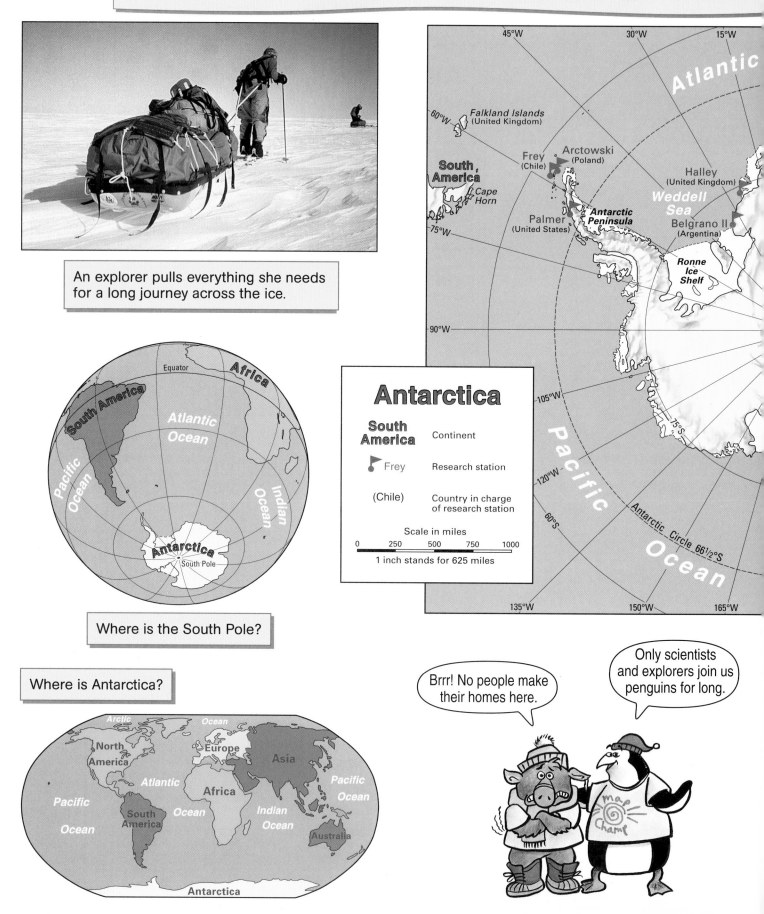

An explorer pulls everything she needs for a long journey across the ice.

Where is the South Pole?

Where is Antarctica?

Antarctica

South America	Continent
Frey	Research station
(Chile)	Country in charge of research station

Scale in miles

0   250   500   750   1000

1 inch stands for 625 miles

Brrr! No people make their homes here.

Only scientists and explorers join us penguins for long.

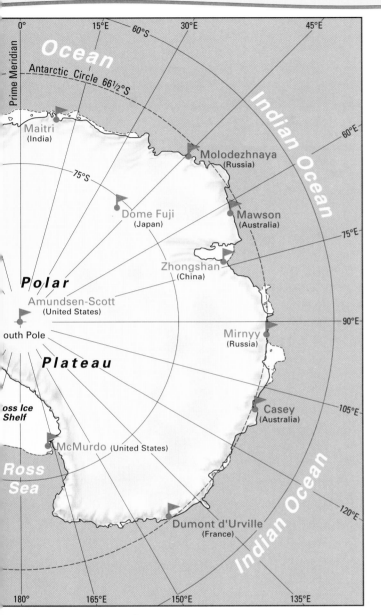

Palmer is an American research station at the edge of Antarctica.

Scientists collect samples of the seawater below an ice shelf.

Penguins gather on the shore and catch the warmth of the sun.

Glossary

A *glossary* is a kind of dictionary.

boundary Imaginary line that separates two states or countries. It is shown as a line on a map.

capital City where the government of a country or state is located.

city Place where many people live and work. A city is bigger than a town.

climate The kind of weather a region usually gets in the course of a year.

compass rose A set of arrows that point north, south, east, and west on a map.

compass rose

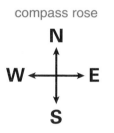

continent One of the seven largest land areas: North America, South America, Africa, Europe, Asia, Australia, and Antarctica.

country A land with one government. Sometimes a country is divided into many states.

desert Dry region with few plants and little rain.

Equator Imaginary line around the middle of the earth. The Equator is the same distance from the North Pole and the South Pole.

Equator

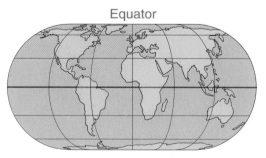

globe A model of the earth that is round like a ball.

hemisphere Any half of the earth. The Northern Hemisphere is north of the Equator.

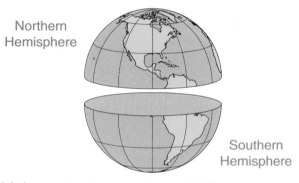

Northern Hemisphere

Southern Hemisphere

highway An important road that connects places that are far apart. Highways are wider than local streets or roads.

key A list that explains the meanings of colors or symbols on a map.

latitude lines East-west lines on a map or globe.

latitude lines

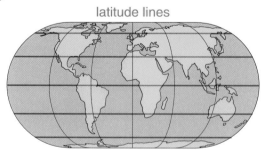

legend The space on a map that gives the map's title and explains its symbols. Sometimes called a *key*.

longitude lines North-south lines on a map or globe.

longitude lines

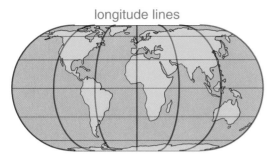

map A special drawing of all or part of the earth as seen from above. A map uses symbols and colors to show where places are located.

mountain Part of the earth that is much taller than the land around it. A mountain is like a hill, but much larger and higher.

national park An area where the land and its plants and animals are protected by the government of the country.

North Pole Imaginary point that is farther north than any other place on earth.

North Pole

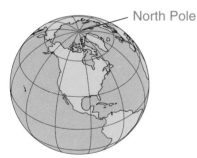

ocean One of the four large, salty bodies of water that cover most of the earth: the Pacific, Atlantic, Indian, and Arctic Oceans.

Prime Meridian A longitude line that passes through London in the United Kingdom. It separates the Western Hemisphere from the Eastern Hemisphere.

Prime Meridian

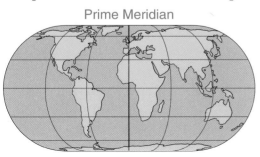

sea A named part of the ocean near land.

South Pole Imaginary point that is farther south than any other place on earth.

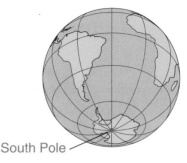

South Pole

sphere A shape that is round like a ball. The earth is a sphere.

state Part of a country. A state has a governor and laws of its own. There are 50 states in the United States of America.

suburb Town or small city that is located near a big city. Most big cities have many suburbs.

swamp A place where plants grow in ground that is covered with shallow water. Sometimes called a *wetland*.

symbol Line, shape, or color that stands for something else. For example, a star on a map may be the symbol for a capital.

town Place where people live and work. A town is smaller than a city.

weather The condition of the air outside. *Windy, sunny,* and *rainy* are some of the words that describe weather.

Now that you know how to use this atlas, you're a Map Champ too!

Index

This index tells you where to find places.

What else does this index tell?